LEARN ABOUT VALUES

PATIENCE

by Cynthia Roberts

Published in the United States of America by The Child's World®
1980 Lookout Drive • Mankato, MN 56003-1705 • 800-599-READ • www.childsworld.com

The Child's World®: Mary Berendes, Publishing Director; Katherine Stevenson, Editor
The Design Lab: Kathy Petelinsek, Art Director; Julia Goozen, Design and Page Production

Photo Credits: © Bob Mitchell/Corbis: 21; © David M. Budd Photography: 7, 9, 11, 13, 17; © Helen King/Corbis: 19;
© Mark Bourdillon/Alamy: 15; © Randy Faris/Corbis: cover; © Roy McMahon/Corbis: 5

Library of Congress Cataloging-in-Publication Data
Roberts, Cynthia, 1960–
  Patience / by Cynthia Roberts.
      p. cm. — (Learn about values)
  ISBN 978-1-59296-673-8 ISBN 1-59296-673-X (library bound: alk. paper)
  1. Honesty—Juvenile literature. 2. Values—Juvenile literature. I. Title. II. Series.
  BJ1533.P3R63 2006
  179'.9—dc22   2006000961

CONTENTS

What Is Patience?

Waiting for something can be hard! You might need to wait for your school bus. You might have to wait in line at the movies. Patience means staying calm while you wait. It means not getting angry or upset.

Patience means staying calm even when something takes a long time.

5

Patience in the Classroom

Sometimes schoolwork can be hard. Maybe you have a question in class. You raise your hand for help. But other students have questions, too. The teacher cannot help everyone at once. You show patience by not waving your arm. You wait calmly until the teacher gets to you.

You can show patience in your classroom by waiting your turn.

Patience **at Home**

Maybe you had a long day at school. But there is some nice new snow outside. Your dad has said he will take you sledding. You would like to go right away! But your dad says you must wait. He needs to shovel the sidewalk first. You show patience by not getting upset.

Patience can mean waiting quietly while someone finishes a job.

9

Patience **and Games**

You are playing a game with your sister. She has never played this game before. You need to **explain** the rules. You must explain them two or three times! You show patience by taking your time. You stay calm while your sister learns how to play.

You can show patience when someone is learning something new.

Patience and Sports

Maybe you like to play hockey. You love to skate fast and try to score. You would like to play the whole game! But there are lots of kids on your team. They all like to play, too. You must sit out while they take turns playing. You show patience by not getting angry. Watching them play can be fun!

Patience means waiting while people take turns.

13

Patience on Vacation

You go on vacation with your family. You are going somewhere far away. It is a long drive. You can hardly wait to get there. You want to go swimming. But you know that getting angry will not get you there faster. You show patience during the drive. You sit quietly and do not get upset.

Sometimes long drives take lots of patience.

Patience **and Lines**

Lines are everywhere! You wait in line to use the slide. You wait in line at the lunchroom. Waiting in line is no fun. Sometimes kids cut in front of others. But you know that is not very nice. You show patience by waiting your turn.

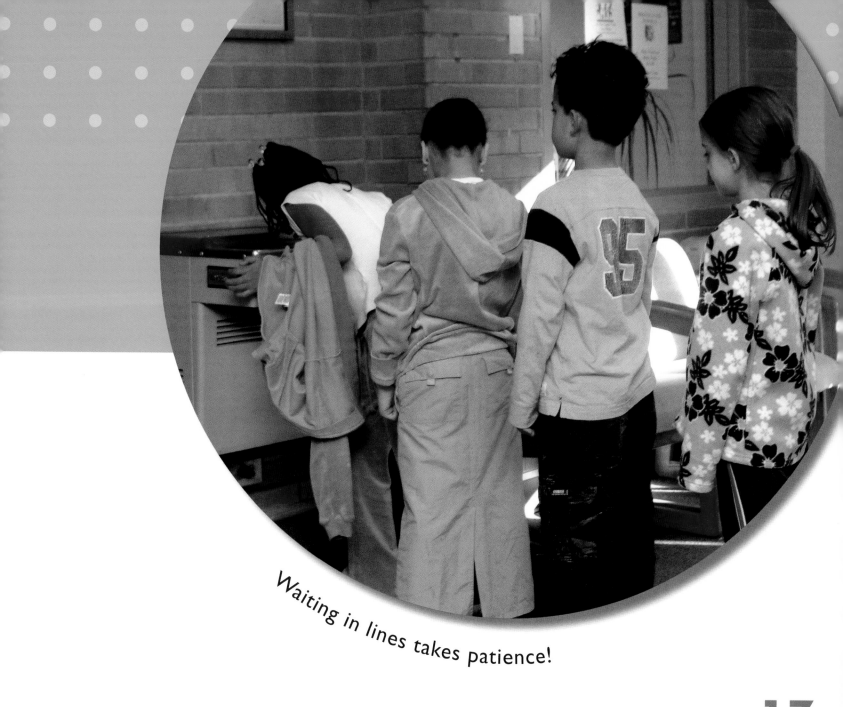

Waiting in lines takes patience!

Patience and You

Learning new things takes patience! Maybe you are learning to play the piano. Maybe you are learning to dance. You make lots of mistakes at first. But you keep **practicing**. You show patience by not getting upset at your mistakes. You keep trying your best. You know you will get better!

It takes patience to learn a new song.

Patience Can Be Hard!

Being patient is not always easy! Sometimes we want things to happen quickly. It is easy to feel upset when they do not. But getting upset makes the wait seem even longer. And getting upset is hard on the people around you. Showing patience is a nicer way to treat the other people. It makes you feel much better, too!

What can you do today to show patience?

glossary

explain
To explain something is to tell how it works.

practicing
Practicing means doing something lots of times so you get better at it.

books

Kyle, Kathryn. *Patience*. Chanhassen, MN: The Child's World, 2002.

Leaney, Cindy. *Summer Vacation: A Story about Patience*. Vero Beach, FL: Rourke, 2003.

Meachen Rau, Dana. *Tired of Waiting*. Minneapolis, MN: Compass Point, 2004.

web sites

Visit our Web page for links about character education and values: *http://www.childsworld.com/links*

Note to parents, teachers, and librarians:
We routinely check our Web links to make sure they're safe, active sites—so encourage your readers to check them out!

index

about the author

Even as a child, Cynthia Roberts knew she wanted to be a writer. She is always working to involve kids in reading and writing, and she loves spending time in the children's section of the library or bookstore. Cynthia enjoys gardening, traveling, and having fun with friends and family.

24